Snowmobiles

BY DENNY VON FINN

TORQUE™

BELLWETHER MEDIA • MINNEAPOLIS, MN

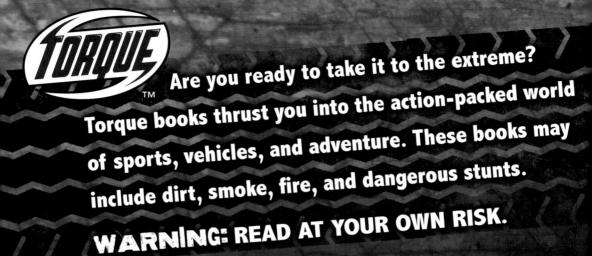

Are you ready to take it to the extreme?
Torque books thrust you into the action-packed world
of sports, vehicles, and adventure. These books may
include dirt, smoke, fire, and dangerous stunts.

WARNING: READ AT YOUR OWN RISK.

This edition first published in 2009 by Bellwether Media, Inc.

No part of this publication may be reproduced in whole or in part without written permission of
the publisher. For information regarding permission, write to Bellwether Media, Inc., Attention:
Permissions Department, Post Office Box 19349, Minneapolis, MN 55419.

Library of Congress Cataloging-in-Publication Data
Von Finn, Denny.
  Snowmobiles / by Denny Von Finn.
    p. cm. — (Torque. Cool rides)
  Includes bibliographical references and index.
  Summary: "Full color photography accompanies engaging information about snowmobiles.
The combination of high-interest subject matter and light text is intended for students in
grades 3 through 7"—Provided by publisher.
  ISBN-13: 978-1-60014-256-7 (hardcover : alk. paper)
  ISBN-10: 1-60014-256-7 (hardcover : alk. paper)
  1. Snowmobiles—Juvenile literature. I. Title.

TL234.2.V66 2009
629.22'042—dc22   2008035639

Contents

What Is a Snowmobile?

A snowmobile is designed to travel well on snow. It runs on a wide **track** that doesn't get stuck in the snow. An engine turns the track to move the snowmobile forward. When the driver turns the handlebars, **skis** on the front of the snowmobile turn side to side.

Snowmobilers can speed up mountainsides or cruise snowy forest trails. Some even enter races against other snowmobiles.

Fast FaCt

Some people call snowmobiles "sleds." Another common name for snowmobiles is "snow machines."

Snowmobile History

Early cars were difficult to drive in the snow. Their thin tires sank easily. In the 1920s, some drivers attached skis and tracks to their cars' tires. This made it much easier to drive in the winter.

An inventor and businessman named Joseph-Armand Bombardier built an early kind of snowmobile in 1937. These large vehicles had skis in front and a track in the back. They had car engines and could seat up to 12 people. Windows and a roof protected the passengers.

In the 1950s, **engineers** discovered ways to make lightweight engines. Smaller snowmobiles were now possible. In 1959, Bombardier's company introduced the Ski-Doo. It was the basic design all future snowmobiles would follow.

Fast FaCt

Some snowmobiles can go more than 120 miles (193 kilometers) per hour.

The Ski-Doo made snowmobiling popular. Several snowmobile companies were founded as more people began snowmobiling. Today, there are four major snowmobile manufacturers and four million snowmobilers in North America.

Parts of a Snowmobile

Modern snowmobiles look and function much differently than earlier models. The driver sits on a seat above the track. He turns handlebars to steer. The engine is in front of the driver. It is covered by a **hood**. A clear windshield on top of the hood protects the driver from wind and flying objects.

Snowmobiles can go very fast because of their powerful engines. Most snowmobiles have a **two-stroke engine**. Two-stroke engines are simple and lightweight.

Some snowmobiles use a **four-stroke engine**. These release less pollution than two-stroke engines. Four-stroke snowmobile engines have less **horsepower** than a two-stroke engine of the same size.

four-stroke engine

The **driveline** uses power from the engine to turn the track. This long rod is attached to wheels that turn the track. Early snowmobile tracks were made of rubber and heavy cloth. Today's tracks are made of a durable material called **Kevlar**.

Snowmobiles in Action

Trail-riding is the most popular type of snowmobiling. The northern United States and Canada offer thousands of miles of remote trails.

Snowmobiles are also used for races called **drags**. There are many types of drags. In hill drags, racers attempt to reach the top of a 500-foot (150-meter) hill before their opponents. Some drags are held without snow. Snowmobilers race on asphalt, grass, and even water!

Other snowmobilers take part in **snocross**. In this fast-paced form of racing, drivers compete on a course full of turns and jumps. Some snocross jumps are more than 30 feet (9 meters) high!

Fast FaCt

The longest cross-country snowmobile race is the Tesoro Iron Dog in Alaska. It is 1,971 miles (3,172 kilometers) long.

Glossary

drags—contests in which racers compete

driveline—a system of shafts that transmits power from the engine to the snowmobile's track

engineers—people who design machines, roads, buildings, and other structures

four-stroke engine—an engine design in which fuel intake, compression, combustion, and exhaust all require a piston stroke

hood—the cover for a snowmobile's engine; hoods are usually made of plastic.

horsepower—a unit for measuring the power of an engine

Kevlar—an extremely strong fabric invented by scientists

skis—the long, board-like extensions under the snowmobile's engine that help keep it atop deep snow and also steer the snowmobile

snocross—a popular form of snowmobile racing in which drivers compete on a course filled with turns and jumps, much like a motocross course

track—the flexible belt beneath the snowmobile driver that propels the snowmobile forward

trail-riding—the most popular form of recreational snowmobiling, in which riders follow groomed, remote trails

two-stroke engine—an engine design in which fuel enters and is compressed with one stroke of the piston; the fuel explodes inside the engine and exhaust gases are released with the second stroke.

To Learn More

AT THE LIBRARY

Doeden, Matt. *Snowmobiles*. Mankato, Minn.: Capstone, 2006.

McClellan, Ray. *Snocross*. Minneapolis, Minn.: Bellwether, 2008.

Sommers, Michael A. *Snowmobiling: Have Fun, Be Smart*. New York: Rosen, 2006.

ON THE WEB

Learning more about snowmobiles is as easy as 1, 2, 3.

1. Go to www.factsurfer.com.

2. Enter "snowmobiles" into the search box.

3. Click the "Surf" button and you will see a list of related Web sites.

With factsurfer.com, finding more information is just a click away.

Index

The images in this book are reproduced through the courtesy of: Yamaha Motor Corporation, front cover, pp. 4-5, 9, 12-13 (lower), 13 (upper), 14 (lower), 14-15 (upper), 16 (small), 18; Associated Press, pp. 6-7; © Photos 12 / Alamy, p. 8; Silvrshootr, p. 10; Glen Gaffney, p. 11; Markus Paulsen / Shazamm/ESPN Image Archive, pp. 16-17; Brad Angus, p. 19 (upper); Doug Pensinger / Staff / Getty Images, pp. 20-21.